Exterminators 2 – Humans 0

Ian Gregory

Illustrated by
Martin Salisbury

Collins Educational
An Imprint of HarperCollins*Publishers*

Published by Collins Educational
77-85 Fulham Palace Road, London W6 8JB

© HarperCollins*Publishers*

ISBN 0 00 323063 5

Illustration, page layout and cover illustration by Martin Salisbury.
Cover design by Clinton Banbury.

Commissioning Editor: Domenica de Rosa
Editor: Paula Hammond
Production: Susan Cashin

Typeset by Harper Phototypesetters Ltd, Northampton, England
Printed by Caledonian International, Glasgow, Scotland

Exterminators 2 – Humans 0

Contents

Chapter 1	Goons on the Moon!	2
Chapter 2	Madness in Moon City	11
Chapter 3	Invasion of the Blobs!	22
Chapter 4	Back from the Dead	27
Chapter 5	Feeding Time!	36
Chapter 6	No Way Out!	48
Chapter 7	Blast Off!	52

To Oonagh

WHY is this savage-looking Thing attacking these two harmless-looking cooks? Was it something they said? Find out in this pulsating, thrill-packed roller-coaster of a book!!

But first, let's back-track to a few days earlier, when our heroes ran into the...

Chapter 1
Goons on the Moon!

Tourists! Welcome to Moon City! A place steeped in history. Moon City...humankind's first city in space. Built by hard-working, pioneer folk, the first Lunar colonists...

...who were unfortunately all killed in the Great Space Plague of 2098. But later, the giant Buzzo-Cola Corporation bought Moon City and turned it into a truly 'out-of-this-world' holiday centre!!

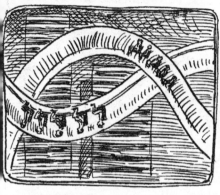

So come to Moon City for the holiday of a lifetime. Enjoy leaping around like a demented kangaroo in the low, low gravity. Take a ride on the old tube-car system, now transformed into the galexy's most exciting roller-coaster ride...

...sample the quaint, traditional food that was eaten by the early colonists, prepared in the old-fashioned way by real human beings!

And remember...you're completely safe under our plasti-glass dome...so no worries about dying a horrible, ghastly death from lack of air, ha ha!

Tourists! I'm fed up with them.

Wheeeee!! Look at me!

There goes another one...

Max, we started out here as tourists remember? Just a couple of weeks' holiday, that's what you said...after all that hard work on Captain Jirk's ship*...and if you hadn't crashed the space limo when we landed here —

You knew I didn't really know how to drive it! Look, we've only been here a few months. We'll soon've saved enough to get a ticket back to Earth, don't worry!

Suddenly...

Are your names Max and Nina?

Come with us, please.

Hang on, that's a gun!

MOVE!

*See 'The Exterminators', still on sale! Get your copy! Stop plugging your last book and get on with it! — Editor.

Just then…

Meanwhile, in the Control Tower, the building which controls Moon City, some pretty strange things are going on too…as the Tower's Manager is about to find out.

Ah, Manager Dribble, sorry to interrupt your game.

Er, that's all right, 'Mr V'!

As you know I've been reducing the number of people working in this building. I hope you don't mind…

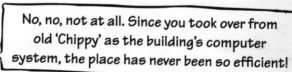

No, no, not at all. Since you took over from old 'Chippy' as the building's computer system, the place has never been so efficient!

GOOD.

I mean, it does seem just a bit odd that I'm the only person left in the building, but…I'm sure you know what you're doing, ha ha! After all, you certainly make the lifts run on time!

Meanwhile, in a hotel room somewhere in Moon City…

I'm Agent Barks, and this is Agent Spencer. We're Weird.

You can say that again!

No, no, we're members of the Weird Files Agency. Our job is to investigate, well, weird stuff. And we need your help.

Back in the Control Tower…

EXIT

Mr Dribble! Not trying to leave us are you?

Er…well…

I'm afraid your card no longer has clearance for this door.

Wait a minute…what's happening?!

Don't you like the scented air?

Aaarghh! Stop! You're suffocating me with 'Lavender Delight'!! Please! Mr V!

Oh, please call me by my real name human filth. I AM VENDOTRON!! And if you want to live, then you'll do exactly as I say.

So VENDOTRON, the mad killer machine, is back! Is he a reformed character, keen to take up gardening, or is he just boringly going to try to take over the world again? Find out in…

Chapter 2
Madness in Moon City

I think there's something weird and sinister going on here on the Moon.

Oh yeah, what?

Er...I don't know. But I've heard rumours. For instance, you know the Buzzo-Cola Corporation owns this city? Well I've found out they've got a secret Cola Research Lab, right under the Control Tower. Who knows what might be going on there?

Oh come off it, how dangerous can experiments with soft drinks be?!

Well how about this then? I've heard that VENDOTRON is involved in...in whatever it is that's going on. And you've met him before, so we thought you could —

You're wrong, VENDOTRON's dead. We killed him!*

* A story told in 'The Extermi
  —still out! yes, yes, all right!

So what do you think?

I think that I haven't been paid for six months. Barks and I get paid by results you see…and we haven't solved a single case yet! So I'm going to make sure we solve this one… EVEN IF IT KILLS YOU!!

GULP!

Well, obviously we'd be happy to help.

Right. You and Barks stay here. You're with me.

Great!

Outside, Max and Agent Spencer are approaching the Tower…

Pretty impressive isn't it?

Yeah, Nina and I wanted to see the view from the top but they wouldn't let us in. Said they were doing the place up…

That's the first thing that made Barks suspicious. Mind you, he also thinks the Tower's really a spaceship in disguise, so I wouldn't pay too much attention to him…

Then what are we doing here??

There still might be something strange going on in there. Anyway Barks has got us these forged passes. They'll open every door. So let's have a look around in there at least.

Using their forged swipe-cards, they enter the lobby…

Busy, isn't it?

Strange. There should be dozens of people working here. Well, the Lab's supposed to be under the Tower. Let's try the lift.

Almost as if we're expected!

Can I go now?

No!

At that moment, not far below their feet, the Tower's Manager has already arrived in the secret Cola Research Lab…

And, minutes later, in a Moon City street…

Meanwhile, underneath the Control Tower…

Suddenly…

Back in the hotel room…

So, is everyone doomed, or what? Find out in…

Chapter 3
Invasion of the Blobs!

Alien monsters! I'm seeing things. It must be a side-effect of those stress pills!

DOWN!

URRPP!

BANG!

They're sticking to the walls! How *do* they do that?

Hang on...I can hear gunfire!

Ah, it's Moon Security. They'll sort 'em out.

But...

Guns have no effect sir! I think they've got, like, really thick skins or something.

What should we do Sir? Sir?

Once out of the hotel, it didn't take Nina and Barks long to find the source of the trouble…

Meanwhile…

And so…

Honestly, the trouble I've had with these service robots. They don't seem to understand that I want them to take over the Moon, not clean floors and cut hair!

Oh really? Er, No.1...I was wondering if you could give me a haircut instead of tying me to this table?

No.1! REMEMBER WHAT I TOLD YOU!

Yeah! Er, over here, human scum!

So what's going to happen to Max? How come VENDOTRON is still alive? And what are those Blob things anyway? Well, don't worry, because everything is explained...er, kind of...in...

26

Chapter 4
Back from the Dead!

Are you sure this is a good idea? This is where those creatures came from, you know!

Look, this has all got something to do with that Tower. Which means that Max and your partner are probably in danger! Don't you care?!

Well...

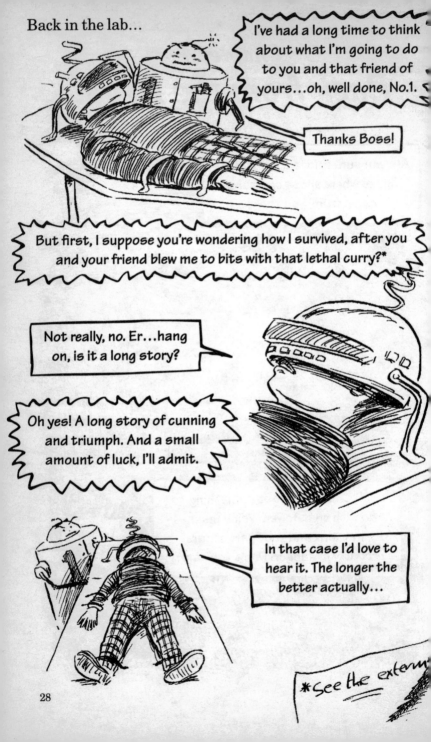

Back in the lab…

I've had a long time to think about what I'm going to do to you and that friend of yours…oh, well done, No.1.

Thanks Boss!

But first, I suppose you're wondering how I survived, after you and your friend blew me to bits with that lethal curry?*

Not really, no. Er…hang on, is it a long story?

Oh yes! A long story of cunning and triumph. And a small amount of luck, I'll admit.

In that case I'd love to hear it. The longer the better actually…

*See the extern

Look, VENDOTRON used to be the head of Zippo-Cola, our arch rivals. Now, forget all that trying to take over the Earth stuff. The point is — not only did that machine have a top business brain, he also knew all Zippo-Cola's secrets — *everything*.

Ah...

Hey! Bring that back!

Later, in the Research Lab...

This is it, all right. OK Chippy you start up-loading data from the chip and analysing it, we'll look at the results after lunch.

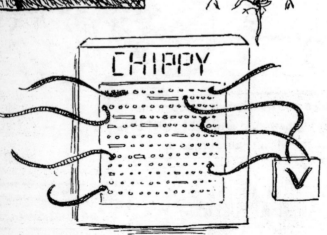

Unluckily for them, the scientists knew a lot about cola, but not too much about computers. They didn't realise that "Chippy",

the building's main computer, was built at a time when people were worried that "smart" buildings might get too intelligent, and go mad and try to take over the world and stuff. Which meant that "Chippy" was about as smart as a potato...

Chippy, look out, there's a computer virus crawling up you! Better shut yourself down!

Oh, blimey!!

So, when the scientists returned from lunch...

I'm sorry ladies and gentlemen. I'm afraid that *I've* taken over this building!

 Well, they're really just huge stomachs. Chemical reactions inside them churn out various products — we just have to feed them the right ingredients.

For instance, cola...

...different types of gum...

Getting them to make strips of chewing gum was more tricky.

And all this is secret? Why?

We didn't think anyone would eat or drink the stuff if they knew where it came from.

HMMM!!!

Is this the end for Max? Or just the start of a whole new career as a Blob? Find out in...

Chapter 5
Feeding Time!

Just as Max is about to be converted into Blob food...

Without its aerial, the robot is cut off from VENDOTRON's control…

Wine...

This way! He'll be controlling the lifts...

LIFT

Gasp! Hang on a minute!

Nearby...

Stop trying to climb the stairs and wait for the lift, you fool!

Where are we going?

The top floor, I found something there while I was trying to find a way out. Come on!

The top floor? Oh, you're kidding...

What's that doing here?

Look, it's some sort of food processor. The ingredients go in there, and it mixes them into a kind of edible slop. I used to use one when I worked in a school canteen on Earth…

Something's activated it! You don't think..?

BEEP!

BEEP!

Having run out of 'fuel' the Blobs are returning.

It's feeding time!

Can't we turn it off?

And be stuck here with a bunch of hungry Blobs?

Sabotage it then? Stop the stuff exploding when it comes out again?

BLEEP
BLEEP

Meanwhile, in the street where Nina and Barks saw their first Blob…

FOOD!!

While…

I don't know what half these chemicals do… Hang on — 'gum Arabic' — I've got an idea! We've got to increase the amount of gum — massively!

Back on the top floor of the Tower…

Round here — I found the computer suite…careful, there's a…

…guard.

42

43

Spencer uses her swipe card to open the door…

In the Lab, Nina and Barks are having problems of their own...

Luckily, at that very moment...

As VENDOTRON is deactivated…The lights flicker…

Up above…

While…

Barks and Nina release the prisoners…

Suddenly…

Zzpt! Click! Buzz! Hello, this is Chippy, the old computer, coming back on line. The emergen cyprogram has now been activated.

'Emergency program

This building has been sealed…

Just before the doors close, a confused and hungry Blob finally reaches the Lab.

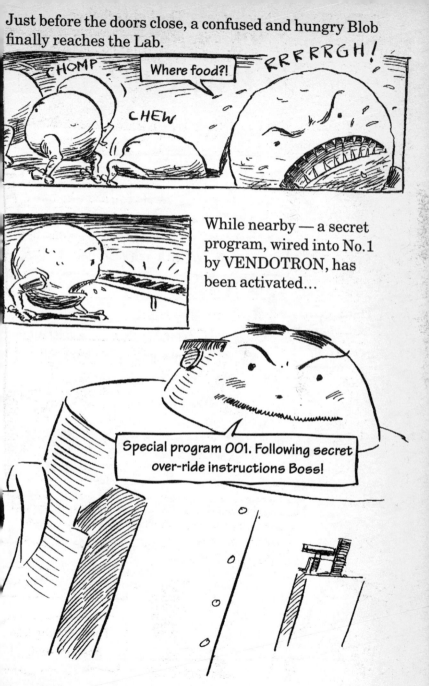

While nearby — a secret program, wired into No.1 by VENDOTRON, has been activated...

Chapter 6
No Way Out!

On the top floor…

In the Tower, a reunion is taking place...

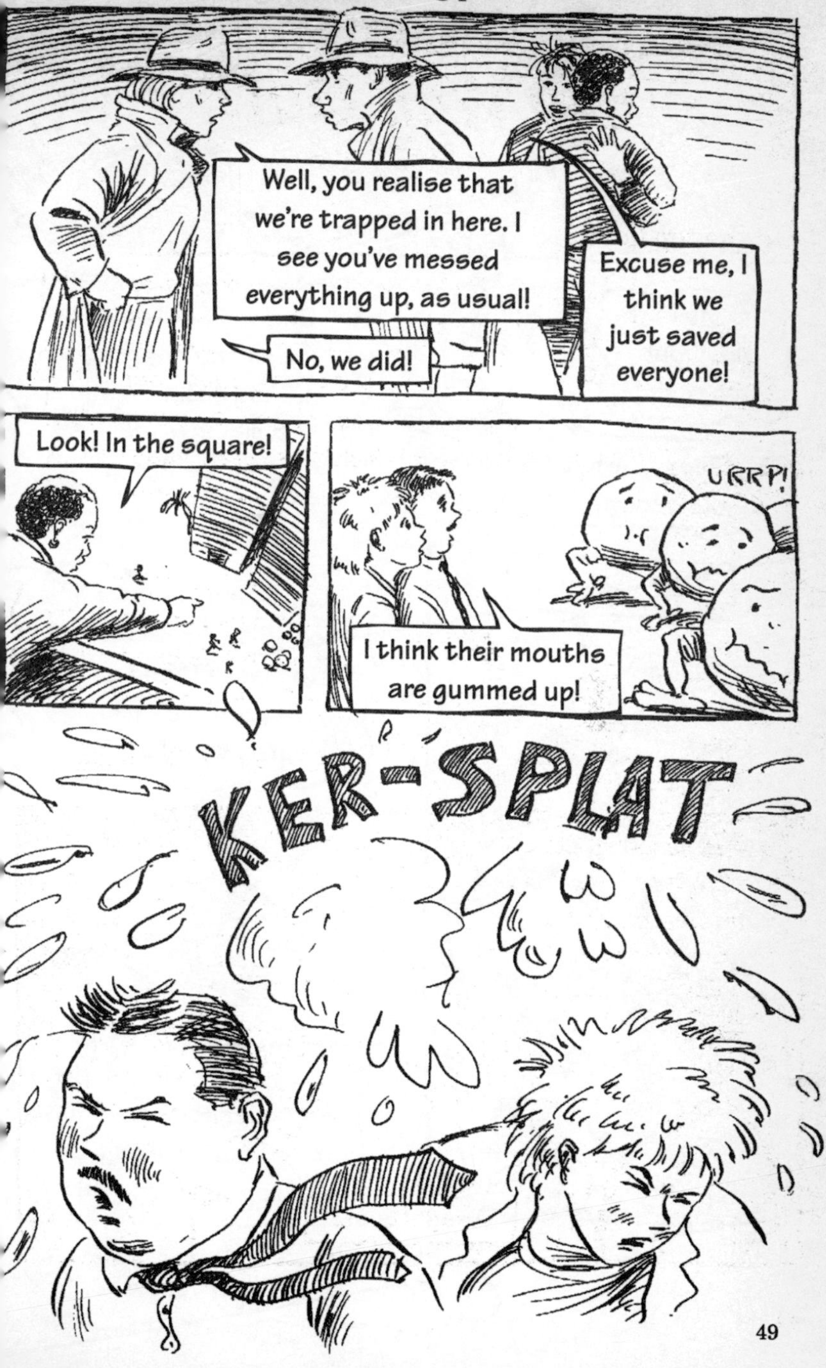

It worked!

Looks like it.

Countdown is about to begin!

Er, Chippy...what countdown?

Oh, I've found out what the emergency program is. You see, this whole building is really a spaceship...

See, I was right!

...and if a disaster hits Moon City, I'm programmed to blast off and get all Buzzo-Cola's people safely back to Earth!

Yeah, great.

Chippy, the disaster is over, and all the staff have b...left the building. So stop the program!

Oh, um, sorry, I don't know how!

51

As the concealed hatch opens, air starts to rush out of Moon City…

While…

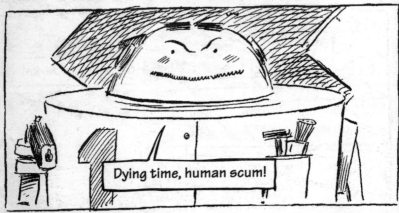

Suddenly...the final Blob arrives!

The air starts to rush out of the room…

Chippy! The door's closing.

Oh yes, well that's an automatic system you see, to stop the whole building losing its air...

Override it! We've got to get out of here!

Ah, well, I'm not sure I'm allowed to do that...

What's happening to the Blob?!

The last Blob, now full of almost nothing but air, starts to expand as the air pressure drops...Then...

POK

Window re-sealed, safe to open door...

This stuff is disgusting...

Did us a favour, though.

So, we still on course for Earth Chippy?

Er...well actually, no. When the air was rushing out it knocked us off-course. But the good news is...

...you can steer us back to Earth?

Er, no, that's the bad news.
I mean, I <u>might</u> be able to. I mean,
probably. If I can find it. No,
the good news is, my drink
dispensers are back on line!
So, nice cup of tea, anyone?
Earl Grey perhaps?
Er...hello? Guys?